AF497692

CRATER LAKE, OREGON.[1]

By J. S. DILLER,
United States Geological Survey.

Of lakes in the United States there are many and in great variety, but of crater lakes there is but one of great importance. Crater lakes are lakes which occupy the craters of volcanoes or pits (calderas) of volcanic origin. They are most abundant in Italy and Central America, regions in which volcanoes are still active; and they occur also in France, Germany, India, Hawaii, and other parts of the world where volcanism has played an important rôle in its geologic history.

The one in the United States belongs to the great volcanic field of the northwest, but it occurs in so secluded a spot among high mountains that it is almost unknown to tourists and men of science who are especially interested in such natural wonders. Crater Lake of southern Oregon lies in the very heart of the Cascade Range, and, while it is especially attractive to the geologist on account of its remarkable geologic history, it is equally inviting to the tourist and others in search of health and pleasure by communion with the beautiful and sublime in nature.

According to W. G. Steel[2] the lake was first seen by white men in 1853. It had long previously been known to the Indians, whose legends have contributed a name, Llao Rock, to one of the prominences of its rim. They regarded the lake with awe as an abode of the Great Spirit. Prospectors were the earliest explorers of the lake.[3] The first travelers of note who visited the lake were Lord Maxwell and Mr. Bentley, who, in 1872, with Capt. O. C. Applegate, of Modoc war fame, and three others, made a boat trip along its borders and named several of the prominences on the rim after members of the party.[4] Mrs. F. F.

---

[1] Published by permission of the Director of the United States Geological Survey. Reprinted from the National Geographic Magazine, February, 1897, Vol. VIII, pages 33–48.

[2] The Mountains of Oregon, by W. G. Steel, 1890, page 13.

[3] The Discovery and Early History of Crater Lake, by M. W. Gorman, Mazama, Vol. I, No. 2, Crater Lake Number, 1897, pages 159. This number contains much valuable information concerning Crater Lake in addition to that referred to.

[4] The names Watchman, Glacier, Llao, and Vidae, which appear on the map of the lake, have recently been adopted by the United States Board on Geographic Names.

SM 97——24

369

192359

Victor saw the lake in 1873, and briefly describes it in "Atlantis Arisen."[1] The same year Mr. S. A. Clarke gave an interesting account of the lake in the December number of the Overland Monthly.

The first Geological Survey party visited the lake in 1883, when Everett Hayden and the writer, after spending several days in examining the rim, tumbled logs over the cliffs to the water's edge, lashed them together with ropes to make a raft, and paddled over to the island. In 1886, under the direction of Capt. (now Maj.) C. E. Dutton, many soundings of the lake were made by W. G. Steel, and a topographic map of the vicinity was prepared by Mark B. Kerr and Eugene Ricksecker. Dutton was the first to discover the more novel and salient features in the geological history of the lake, of which he has given, for his entertaining pen, an all too brief account.[2]

Under the inspiration of the "Mazamas," a society of mountain climbers at Portland, Oregon,[3] a more extended study of the lake has just been made by Government parties from the Department of Agriculture, the Fish Commission, and the Geological Survey.

Crater Lake is deeply set in the summit of the Cascade Range, about 65 miles north of the California line. As yet it may be reached only by private conveyance over about 80 miles of mountain roads from Ashland, Medford, or Gold Hill, on the Southern Pacific Railroad, in the Rogue River Valley of southern Oregon (see fig. 1). This valley marks the line between the Klamath Mountains of the Coast Range on the west and the Cascade Range on the east. The journey from the railroad to Crater Lake affords a good opportunity to observe some of the most important features of this great pile of lavas. The Cascade Range in southern Oregon is a broad irregular platform, terminating rather abruptly in places upon its borders, especially to the westward, where the underlying Cretaceous and Tertiary sediments come to the surface. It is surmounted by volcanic cones and coulees, which are generally smooth, but sometimes rough and rugged. The cones vary greatly in size and are distributed without regularity. Each has been an active volcano. The fragments blown out by violent eruption have fallen about the volcanic orifice from which they issued and built up cinder cones. From their bases have spread streams of lava (coulees), raising the general level of the country between the cones. From some vents by many eruptions, both explosive and effusive, large cones, like Pitt, Shasta, and Hood have been built up. Were we to examine their internal structure, exposed in the walls of the canyons carved in their slopes, we should find them composed of overlapping layers of lava and volcanic conglomerate, a structure which is well illustrated in the rim of Crater Lake.

---

[1] "Atlantis Arisen," by Mrs. Francis Fuller Victor, page 179.

[2] Science, Vol. VII, 1886, pages 179–182, and Eighth Annual Report of the United States Geological Survey, pages 156–159.

[3] The National Geographic Magazine, Vol. VIII, 1897, page 58.

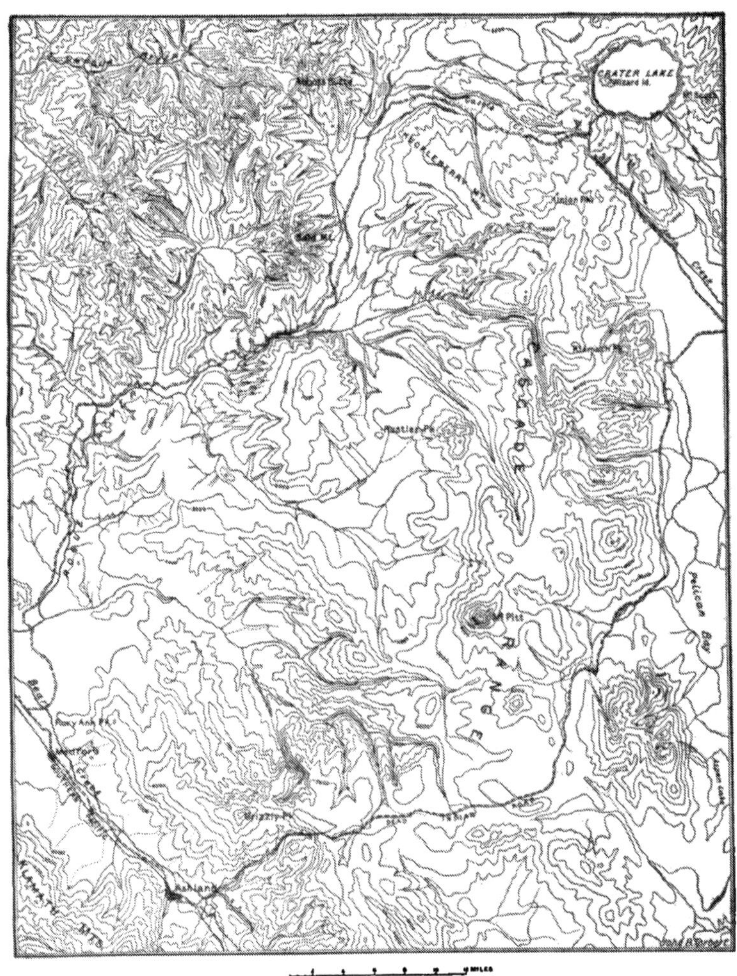

FIG. 1.—MAP SHOWING ROUTES TO CRATER LAKE FROM ASHLAND AND MEDFORD ON THE OREGON AND CALIFORNIA LINE OF THE SOUTHERN PACIFIC RAILROAD.

Reduced from United States Geological Survey Ashland Sheet, Oregon.

The journey from Ashland by the Dead Indian road crosses the range where the average altitude is less than 5,000 feet. The road passes within a few miles of Mount Pitt and skirts Pelican Bay of Klamath Lake, famous for its fishing. After following northward for some 20 miles along the eastern foot of the range, it ascends the eastern slope, along the castled canyon of Anna Creek to the rim of Crater Lake.

From Medford or Gold Hill, the trip is a trifle shorter by the Rogue River road. It affords some fine views of the canyons and rapids of that turbulent stream and of the high falls, where it receives its affluents. Striking features along both roads, within 20 miles of the lake, are the plains developed upon a great mass of detritus filling the valleys. Across these plains Anna Creek and Rogue River have carved deep, narrow canyons with finely sculptured walls, which the roads follow for some distance.

Approaching the lake from any side, the observer sees, as in the distant part of figure 2, a broad cluster of gentle peaks rising about a thousand feet above the general crest of the range on which they stand, but not until after he has left the main road, 3 miles from the lake, does he begin to feel the steepness of the ascent. The way winds over a large moraine littered with lava bowlders and well studded with firs. Arriving at the crest, the lake in all its majestic beauty, as it appears in figure 3, comes suddenly upon the scene, and is profoundly impressive. Descending the wooded slope a short distance within the rim to Victor Rock, an excellent general view of the lake is obtained. Upon the left is the western border of the lake (fig. 4), and upon the right its southern border (fig. 5). The eye beholds 20 miles of unbroken cliffs ranging from over 500 to nearly 2,000 feet in height, encircling a deep blue sheet of placid water, in which the mirrored walls vie with the originals in brilliancy and greatly enhance the depth of the prospect.

The first point to fix our fascinated gaze is Wizard Island, lying nearly 2 miles away, near the western margin of the lake. Its irregular western edge and the steep but symmetrical truncated cone in the eastern portion are very suggestive of volcanic origin. We can not, however, indulge our first impulse to go at once to the island, for the various features of the rim are of greater importance in unraveling the earlier stages of its geological history.

The outer and inner slopes of the rim are in strong contrast; while the one is gentle, ranging in general from 10° to 15°, the other is abrupt and full of cliffs. This difference is well expressed by the contour map in figure 6. The vertical interval of the contours is 200 feet. Upon the inner slope the contours are crowded close together to show a slope so steep that one needs to travel but a little way to descend 200 feet, while upon the outer slope the contours are so far apart that to descend 200 feet one needs to travel a considerable portion of a mile. The outer slope at all points is away from the lake, and as the rim rises at least 1,000 feet above the general summit of the range, it is evidently the basal portion of a great hollow cone in which the lake is contained.

In addition to the strong contrast between the outer and inner slopes of the rim the map shows the occurrence of a number of small cones upon the outer slope of the great cone. These adnate cones are of peculiar significance when we come to consider the volcanic rocks of which the region is composed. The rim is ribbed by ridges and spurs radiating from the lake, and the head of each spur is marked by a prominence on the crest of the rim. The variation in the altitude of the rim crest is 1,460 feet (from 6,759 to 8,228) with seven points rising above 8,000 feet. The crest generally is passable, so that a pedestrian may follow it continuously around the lake, with the exception of short intervals about the notches in the southern side. At many points the best going is on the inner side of the crest, where the open slope, generally well marked with deer trails over beds of pumice, affords an unobstructed view of the lake.

Reference has already been made to the glacial phenomena of the outer slope of the rim. There are scattered bowlders upon the surface, and also in piles of glacial moraine (fig. 7) which contain besides bowlders much gravel and sand. Such glacial drift is spread far and wide over the southern and western portion of the rim, extending down the watercourses in some cases for miles to broad plains through which the present streams have carved the deep and picturesque canyons already observed on the ascent. At many points the lavas are well rounded, smoothed, and striated by glacial action. This is true of the ridges as well as of the valleys, and the distribution of these marks is coextensive with that of the glacial detritus.

A feature that is particularly impressive to the geologist making a trip around the lake on the rim crest is the general occurrence of polished and striated rocks, in place on the very brow of the cliff overlooking the lake. The best displays are along the crest for 3 miles northwest of Victor Rock, but they occur also on the slopes of Llao Rock, Round Top, Kerr Notch, and Eagle crags, thus completing the circuit of the lake. On the adjacent slope toward the lake the same rocks present rough fractured surfaces, showing no striæ. The glaciation of the rim is a feature of its outer slope only, but as shown in figure 8, it reaches up to the very crest. The glaciers armed with stones in their lower parts, that striated the crown of the rim, must have come down from above, and it is evident that the topographic conditions of to-day afford no such source of supply. The formation of glaciers requires an elevation extending above the snow line to afford a gathering ground for the snow that it may accumulate, and under the influence of gravity descend to develop glaciers lower down on the mountain slopes. During the glacial period Crater Lake did not exist. Its site must then have been occupied by a mountain to furnish the conditions necessary for the extensive glaciation of the rim, and the magnitude of the glacial phenomena indicates that the peak was a large one, rivaling, apparently, the highest peaks of the range.

The Mazamas held a meeting in August, 1896, at Crater Lake in connection with the Crater Lake clubs of Medford, Ashland, and Klamath Falls, of the same State. Recognizing that the high mountain which once occupied the place of the lake was nameless, they christened it, with appropriate ceremonies, Mount Mazama. The rim of the lake is a remnant of Mount Mazama, but when the name is used in this paper reference is intended more especially to that part which has disappeared.

The inner slope of the rim, so well in view from Victor Rock, although precipitous, is not a continuous cliff. It is made up of many cliffs, whose horizontal extent is generally much greater than the vertical. The cliffs are in ledges, and sometimes the whole slope from crest to shore is one great cliff, not absolutely vertical, it is true, but yet at so high an angle as to make it far beyond the possibility of climbing. Dutton Cliff on the southern and Llao Rock on the northern borders of the lake are the greatest cliffs of the rim. Besides cliffs, the other elements of the inner slope are forests and talus, and these make it possible at a few points to approach the lake, not with great ease, but yet, care being taken, with little danger. Southwest of the lake the inner slope, clearly seen from Victor Rock, is pretty well wooded, and from near the end of the road, just east of Victor Rock, a steep trail descends to the water. Where fresh talus slopes prevail there are no trees, and the loose material maintains the steepest slope possible without sliding. Such slopes are well displayed along the western shore opposite the island and near the northeast corner of the lake under the palisades, illustrated in figure 10. At this point the rim is only 520 feet high, and a long slide, called from its shape the Wineglass, reaches from crest to shore.

The best views of the rim are obtained from a boat on the lake, which affords an opportunity to examine in detail the position and structure of the cliffs. They are composed wholly of volcanic conglomerate and streams of lava arranged in layers that dip into the rim and away from the lake on all sides. Both forms of volcanic material are well exposed on the trail descending the inner slope, and, although most of the cliffs are of lava, many are of conglomerate.

On arriving at the water's edge the observer is struck with the fact that there is no beach. The steep slopes above the surface of the lake continue beneath its waters to great depths. Here and there upon the shore, where a rill descends from a melting snow bank near the crest, a small delta deposit makes a little shallow, turning the deep-blue water to pale green.

As the boat skirts the western shore and passes toward Llao Rock, the layered structure of the rim is evident. This feature is best illus-trated in figure 4. On the whole, the lava streams predominate. although there is much conglomerate. Of all the flows exposed upon the inner slope, that of Llao Rock is most prominent and interesting. In the middle it is over 1,200 feet thick, and fills an ancient valley down the outer slope of the rim. Upon either side it tapers to a thin edge against the upper slope of the valley. Figure 11, from a color sketch of the photograph from which figure 3 was prepared, shows the Llao Rock flow distinctly. To the lake it presents a sheer cliff—that is, it is abruptly cut off—and one wonders how much farther it may have extended in that direction. Beneath the rock the outline of the valley in cross section is evident, and it rests upon many layers of older lavas forming the rim down to the water's edge. The direction of flow in this great lava stream forces us to believe that it was erupted from a large volcano which once stood upon the site of the lake. Every layer of lava in the rim is a coulee, dipping away from the lake. This is especially well shown in the canyon of Sun Creek, cut in its outer slope. The sections of these radiating flows exposed upon the inner slope of the rim all tell the same story as to their source. By projecting the lavas in their course toward a common center we can reconstruct in fancy the great volcano, Mount Mazama, which once occupied the place of the lake, and, like Shasta or Rainier, formed a great landmark of the region. Proceeding eastward from Llao Rock the rim loses somewhat in height, and at the head of Cleetwood Cove one sees the remarkable spectacle of a lava stream descending the inner slope of the rim. It is the only one that has behaved in this way, and its action throws much light upon the disappearance of Mount Mazama.

The Palisades are less than 600 feet in elevation above the lake, and are composed almost wholly of one great flow. The streams of lava extending northeast from this portion of the rim are broad and much younger in appearance than those forming the great cliffs south of the lake, where the flows are thinner and more numerous.

Round Top is a dome-shaped hill over the eastern end of the Palisades, and is made up chiefly of the lava stream that formed the Palisades, overlain by two sheets of pumice separated by a layer of rhyolite. The upper surface of the Palisade flow, where best exposed upon the lakeward slope of Round Top, bears glacial striæ, that extend beneath the layers of pumice and rhyolite of later eruption from Mount Mazama. It is evident from this relation that Mount Mazama was an active volcano during the glacial period. The occurrence of eruptions from a snow-capped volcano must necessarily produce great floods, and these conditions may account in some measure at least for the detritus-filled valleys of the streams rising on the rim of Crater Lake.

Returning from this glacial digression to the boat trip on the lake, it is observed upon the eastern side of the lake that Red Cloud Cliff is rendered beautiful by the pinnacles of reddish tuff near the summit, where it is capped by a great, dark flow of rhyolite, filling a valley in the older rim and extending far to the northeast. Here the springs begin to gush from the inner slope and cascade their foaming rills to the lake. They recur at Sentinel Rock, Dutton Cliff, and especially under Eagle Crag, as well as farther westward. Their sources in many cases can be seen in the banks of snow above, but in others they gush forth as real springs, whose water must find its way in from the snow upon the outer slope.

The boldest portion of the rim, excepting perhaps Llao Rock, is Dutton Cliff, which is made more impressive by the deep U-shape notches on either s de and the Phantom Ship at its foot (fig. 12). The notches mark poin where the canyons of Sun and Sand creeks pass through the rim to the cliff overlooking the lake. In figure 13, which shows the same view as figure 12, but in the opposite direction, the notch at the head of Sun Creek Canyon is well illustrated. These canyons, due to erosion on lines of drainage, belong to the period when the topographic conditions in that region were quite unlike those of to-day. They were carved out by streams of ice and water descending from a point over the lake, and their presence, ending as they do in the air hundreds of feet above the present water level, affords strong evidence in favor of the former reality of Mount Mazama.

The Phantom Ship (fig. 14) is a craggy little islet near the border of the lake under Dutton Cliff. Its rugged hull, with rocks towering like the masts of a ship, suggests the name, and, phantom-like, it disappears when viewed in certain lights from the western rim. Standing in line with an arête that descends from an angle of the cliff, it possibly marks a continuation of the sharp spur beneath the water, or perhaps, but much less likely, it is a block slid down from the cliff. Whatever its history, it attracts everyone by its beauty and winsomeness.

At times of volcanic eruption the lava rises within the volcano until it either overflows the crater at the top or, by the great pressure of the column, bursts open the sides of the volcano and escapes through the fissure to the surface. In the latter case, as the molten material cools, the fissure becomes filled with solid lava and forms a dike. The best example of this sort about Crater Lake appears along the inner slope directly north of Wizard Island, and is locally known as the Devil's Backbone. It is shown in figures 3 and 11 across the left end of Wizard Island. This dike rock, standing on edge, varies from 5 to 25 feet in thickness and cuts the rim from water to crest. Dikes are most numerous in the older portion of the rim under Llao Rock. They do not cut up through Llao Rock and are clearly older than the lava of which that rock is formed. Dikes occur at intervals all around the lake and radiate from it, suggesting that the central volcanic vent from which they issued must have been Mount Mazama.

There is another important feature concerning the kinds of volcanic rocks and their order of eruption and distribution about the rim of Crater Lake that is of much interest to the geologist. All the older lavas comprising the inner slope of the rim, especially toward the water's edge, are andesites. The newer ones, forming the top of the rim in Llao Rock, Round Top, and the Rugged Crest about the head of Cleetwood Cove as well as at Cloud Cap, are rhyolites. Other later

flows, all of which escaped from the smaller adnate cones upon th
outer slope of the rim, are basalts. The eruptions began with lava
containing a medium amount of silica (andesites), and after long
continued activity lavas both richer (rhyolites) and poorer (basalts) i
silica follow, giving a completeness to the products of this great vo
canic center that make it an interesting field of study. Furthermore
the remarkable opportunity afforded by the dissected volcano for th
examination of its structure and succession of lavas is unsurpassed
It should be stated, before dismissing the kinds of lava, that there are
some rhyolites in the Sun Creek Canyon south of the lake that appear
to be older than those upon the north side, and that the final lava of
the region on Wizard Island is andesite.

The glaciation and structure of the rim clearly establish the former
existence of Mount Mazama, but there may well be doubt as to its
exact form and size. Judging from the fact that Mount Shasta and
the rim of Crater Lake have the same diameter at an altitude of 8,000
feet, and that their lavas are similar, it may with some reason be inferred
that Mount Mazama and Mount Shasta were nearly of equal height.
The slopes of Mount Shasta may be somewhat steeper than those of
the rim of Crater Lake at an equal altitude, but the glaciation of the
rim is such as to require a large peak for its source.

In figure 9 is given a section of Crater Lake and its rim, with the
probable ou 'ine of Mount Mazama. Wonderful as the lake, encircled
by cliffs, ma, serves but to conceal in part the greatest wonder—
that is, the enormous pit or caldera which is half filled by the lake.
The caldera is 4,000 feet deep. An impressive illustration of it is seen
in figure 15 which was prepared from a photograph of a model of
Crater Lake now in the United States National Museum. The water
surface is represented by glass, so that one may see through to the
bottom and get the full impression of the depth of this tremendous
hole in the ground. It extends from the top of the rim, which is
the very summit of the Cascade Range, halfway down to the sea level,
and nearly a square mile of its bottom is below the level of Upper
Klamath Lake at the eastern foot of the range. The volume of the
caldera is nearly a dozen cubic miles, and if we add the volume of the
lost Mount Mazama, that amount would be increased by at least one-
half. How was it possible to remove so large a mass and in the process
develop so great a depression?

The caldera is completely inclosed, so that it can not be regarded as
an effect of erosion. The volcanic origin of everything about the lake
would suggest in a general way that this great revolution must have
been wrought by volcanism, either blown out by a great volcanic explosion or swallowed up by an equally great engulfment. It is well known
that pits have been produced by volcanic explosions, and some of them
are occupied by lakes of the kind usually called crater lakes. Depres-
sions produced in this way, however, are, with rare exceptions, sur-

rounded by rims composed of the fragmental material blown out from the depression.

At first sight the rim about Crater Lake suggests that the caldera was produced by an explosion, and the occurrence of much pumice in that region lends support to this preliminary view; but on careful examination we find, as already stated, that the rim is not made up of fragments blown from the pit, but of layers of solid lava interbedded with those of volcanic conglomerate erupted from Mount Mazama before the caldera originated. The moraines deposited by glaciers descending from the mountain formed the surface around a large part of the rim, and as there is no fragmental deposits on these moraines, it is evident that there is nothing whatever to indicate any explosive action in connection with the formation of the caldera.

We may be aided in understanding the possible origin of the caldera by picturing the conditions that must have obtained during an effusive eruption of Mount Mazama. At such a time the column of molten material rose in the interior of the mountain until it overflowed at the summit or burst open the sides of the mountain and escaped through fissures. Fissures formed in this way usually occur high on the slopes of the mountain. If instead, however, an opening were effected on the mountain side at a much lower level—say some thousands of feet below the summit—and the molten material escaped, the mountain would be left hollow, and the summit, having so much of its support removed, might cave in and disappear in the molten reservoi..

Something of this sort is described by Professor Dana as occurring at Kilauea, in Hawaii. The lake in that case is not water, but molten lava, for Kilauea is yet an active volcano. In 1840 there was an eruption from the slopes of Kilauea, 27 miles distant from the lake and over 4,000 feet below its level. The column of lava represented by the lake of molten material in Kilauea sank away in connection with this eruption to a depth of 385 feet, and the floor of the region immediately surrounding the lake, left without support, tumbled into the depression. In the intervals between eruptions the molten column rises again toward the surface, only to be lowered by subsequent eruptions, and the subsidence is not always accompanied by an outflow of lava upon the surface. Sometimes, however, it gushes forth as a great fountain a hundred feet or more in height.

The elevated position of the great caldera occupied by Crater Lake makes its origin by subsidence seem the more probable. The level of the lowest bed of the lake reaches the surface within 15 miles down the western slope of the range. That Mount Mazama was ingulfed is plainly suggested by the behavior of its final lava stream. The greater portion of this last flow descended and spread over the outer slope of the rim, but from the thickest part of the flow where it fills an old valley at the head of Cleetwood Cove some of the same lava, as already noted, poured down the inner slope. The only plausible explanation

of this phenomena seems to be that soon after the final eruption of
Mount Mazama, and before the thickest part of the lava effused at that
time had solidified, the mountain collapsed and sank away and the yet
viscous portion of the stream followed down the inner slope of the
caldera.

It has been suggested, but perhaps not in serious thought, that the
cone on Wizard Island may represent the summit of the sunken Mount
Mazama projecting above the water. To determine the truth of the
matter we must cross over to the island. Wizard Island has two por-
tions—an extremely rough lava field and a cinder cone. These parts
may be distinguished in figure 16, a view of the island from the
Watchman. A portion of the lava field is shown in the foreground of
figure 18. The lava is dark and has a much more basaltic look than
any seen in the main body of the rim. It has evidently been erupted
from the base of the cinder cone in its present position. The cinder
cone, too, is a perfect little volcano, with steep symmetrical slopes. 845
feet in height, and surmounted by a crater 80 feet deep. A portion of
this crater is shown in figure 17. It is so new and fresh that it
is scarcely forested, and shows no trace of weathering. Instead of
being a part of the sunken Mount Mazama, it is an entirely new volcano built up since the subsidence by volcanic action upon the bottom
of the caldera. Were it not for the lake the whole bottom of the
caldera could be examined, and it is possible that other small volcanic
cones might be found. This suggestion is borne out by the soundings
of the lake, which appear to reveal two other cases, but they do not
rise to within 400 feet of the surface of the water. It is evident that
the volcanic eruptions upon the bottom of the caldera have partially
filled it up. Originally it may have been much more than 4,000 feet
deep.

Given the caldera with water-tight walls, there is no difficulty in
forming Crater Lake, for in that region precipitation is greater than
evaporation. Observations upon precipitation and evaporation have
not been made at Crater Lake, but, judging from those made at nearest
points, the annual precipitation should be between 60 and 70 inches,
while the annual evaporation is between 50 and 60 inches. The average diameter of the lake is nearly 5 miles. Its area, including Wizard
Island, is about 21.30 square miles. The drainage area inclosed by the
rim of the lake, according to Mr. E. C. Barnard, is 27.48 square miles.
During the winter great masses of snow drift within the rim, and thus
considerably augment the normal precipitation of the lake. The lake
does not fill up and overflow. The surplus water must have a subterra-
nean outlet, probably toward the southeast, where the region is tra-
versed by extensive breaks in the rocks, and abounds in excellent
springs.

The color of the lake is deep blue, excepting along the borders, where
it merges into various shades and tints of green. It is so transparent

that even on a hazy day a white dinner plate 10 inches in diameter may be seen at a depth of nearly 100 feet. It contains no fish, but a small crustacean flourishes in its waters, and salamanders occur in abundance locally along the shore.

The level of the lake oscillates with the seasons. During the rainy winter it rises, and in the summer it falls. In August, 1896, observations were made for twenty-two days, and the lake sank at the rate of 1 inch for every five or six days, depending somewhat on the conditions of the weather. The Mazamas have established a water gauge, and it was hoped that an extended series of observations would be obtained, but the ice broke it off the next winter.

Mr. B. W. Evermann, of the United States Fish Commission, who visited the lake last summer, made some interesting observations of its temperature. At 1 p. m., August 22—

The temperature of the surface water was .... 60°
At a depth of 555 feet the temperature was .... 39°
At a depth of 1,043 feet the temperature was .... 41°
At a depth of 1,623 feet (on the bottom) the temperature was .... 46°

The increase of temperature with the depth suggests that the bottom may yet be warm from volcanic heat, but more observations are needed to fully establish such an abnormal relation of temperatures in a body of water.

Aside from its attractive scenic features, Crater Lake affords one of the most interesting and instructive fields for the study of volcanic geology to be found anywhere in the world. Considered in all its aspects, it ranks with the Grand Canyon of the Colorado, the Yosemite Valley, and the Falls of Niagara, and it is interesting to note that a bill has been introduced in Congress to make it a national park for the pleasure and instruction of the people.

FIG. 2.—RIM OF CRATER LAKE IN THE DISTANCE, AS SEEN FROM THE SOUTH, ACROSS THE CANYON OF ANNA CREEK.

From a photograph by J. S. Diller.

FIG. 3.—CRATER LAKE, OREGON. WIZARD ISLAND, DEVILS BACKBONE, AND LLAO ROCK IN THE DISTANCE.
From a photograph by M. M. Hazeltine.

Fig. 4.—Southwestern Border of Crater Lake. Victor Rock in the Foreground. The Watchman and Glacier Peak in the Distance.

From a photograph by Maj. C. E. Dutton.

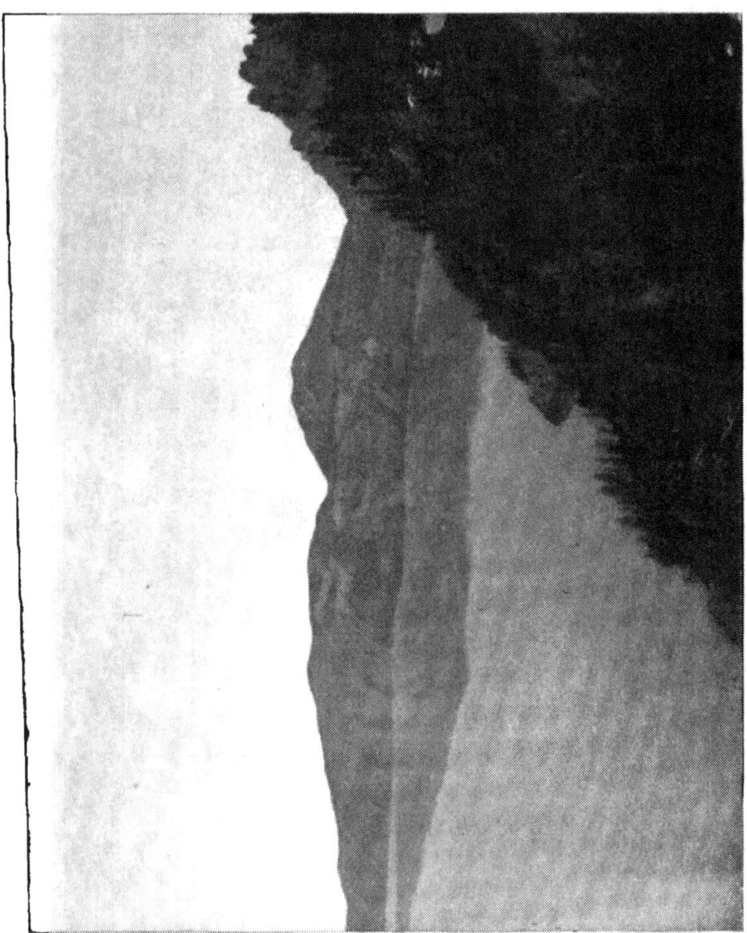

FIG. 5.—SOUTHERN BORDER OF CRATER LAKE. MOUNT SCOTT IN THE DISTANCE.

From a photograph by Maj. C. E. Dutton.

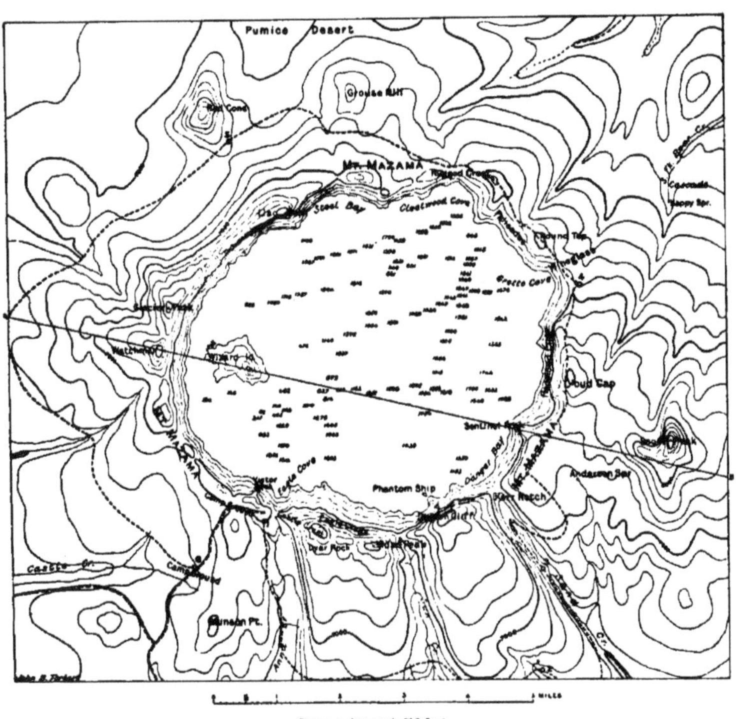

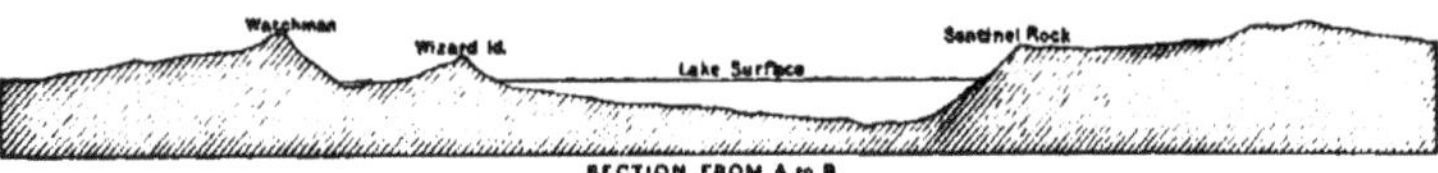

(Reduced from U. S. Geological Survey special sheet.)

FIG. 6.—MAP OF CRATER LAKE.

(Soundings in feet.)

Feasible pack trail around the lake shown thus: ...., not blazed.
Camping places shown thus: o

FIG. 7.—GLACIAL MORAINE NEAR CAMP GROUND, CRATER LAKE.

From a photograph by J. S. Diller.

FIG. 8.—GLACIATED CREST OF RIM OF CRATER LAKE.
From a photograph by M. M. Hazeltine.

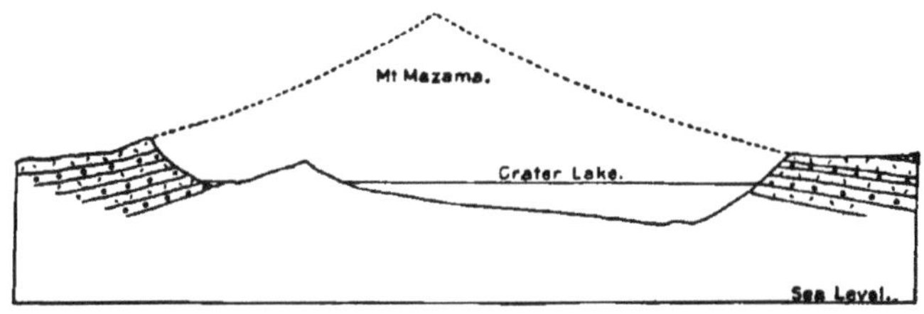

FIG. 9.—SECTION OF CRATER LAKE AND ITS RIM, WITH THE PROBABLE OUTLINE
OF MOUNT MAZAMA. STRUCTURAL DETAILS GENERALIZED.
Vertical and horizontal scales the same.

FIG. 10.—THE PALISADES, ROUND TOP, AND WINEGLASS SLIDE ON NORTHEAST BORDER OF CRATER LAKE.

From a photograph by J. S. Diller.

FIG. 11.—CRATER LAKE. THE DEVILS BACKBONE AND LLAO ROCK SEEN BEYOND WIZARD ISLAND. THE SHARP POINT OF MOUNT THIELSON APPEARS IN THE DISTANCE.

FIG. 12.—SOUTHERN SHORE OF CRATER LAKE FROM KERRS NOTCH (LOOKING WEST).

From a photograph by J. S. Diller.

FIG. 13.—SOUTHERN SHORE OF CRATER LAKE FROM CASTLE CREST. MOUNT SCOTT AND PHANTOM SHIP ON THE LEFT; NOTCH AT THE HEAD OF SUN CREEK ON THE RIGHT.

From a photograph by H. B. Patton.

FIG. 14.—THE PHANTOM SHIP.

From photograph, by permission of C. C. Lewis.

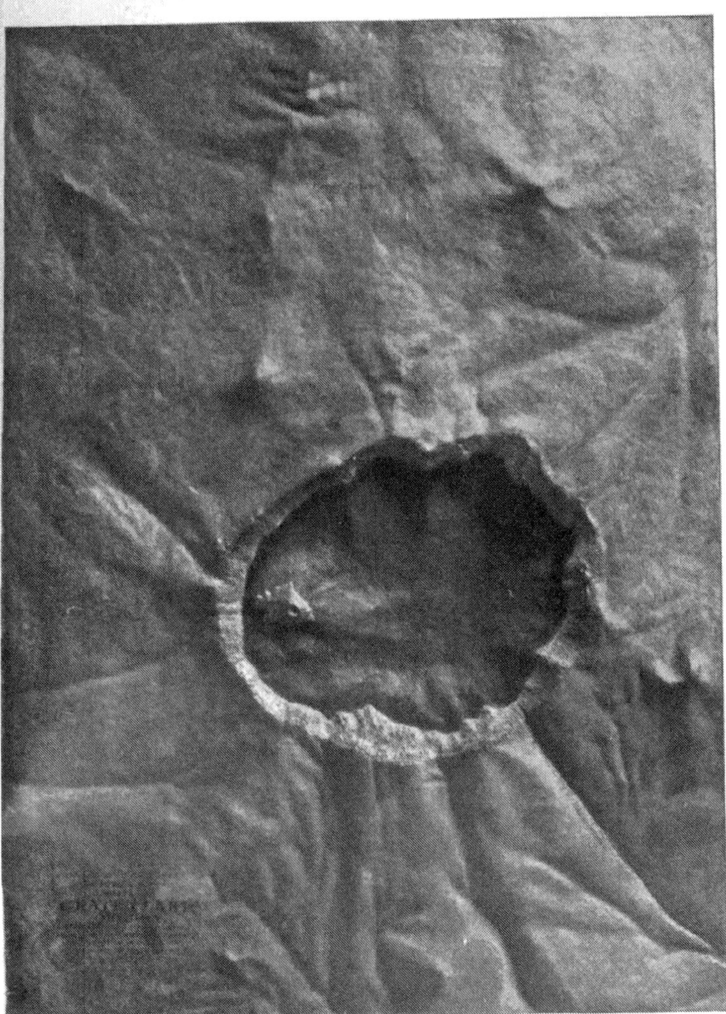

FIG. 15.—CRATER LAKE AS IT WOULD APPEAR FROM A HEIGHT OF OVER 20 MILES ABOVE IT.

Prepared from a photograph of a relief model in the U. S. National Museum.

FIG. 16.—WIZARD ISLAND, FROM THE WATCHMAN.
From a photograph by M. M. Hazeltine.

FIG. 17.—SNOWDRIFT IN THE CRATER OF THE CINDER CONE ON WIZARD ISLAND.
From a photograph by H. B. Patton.

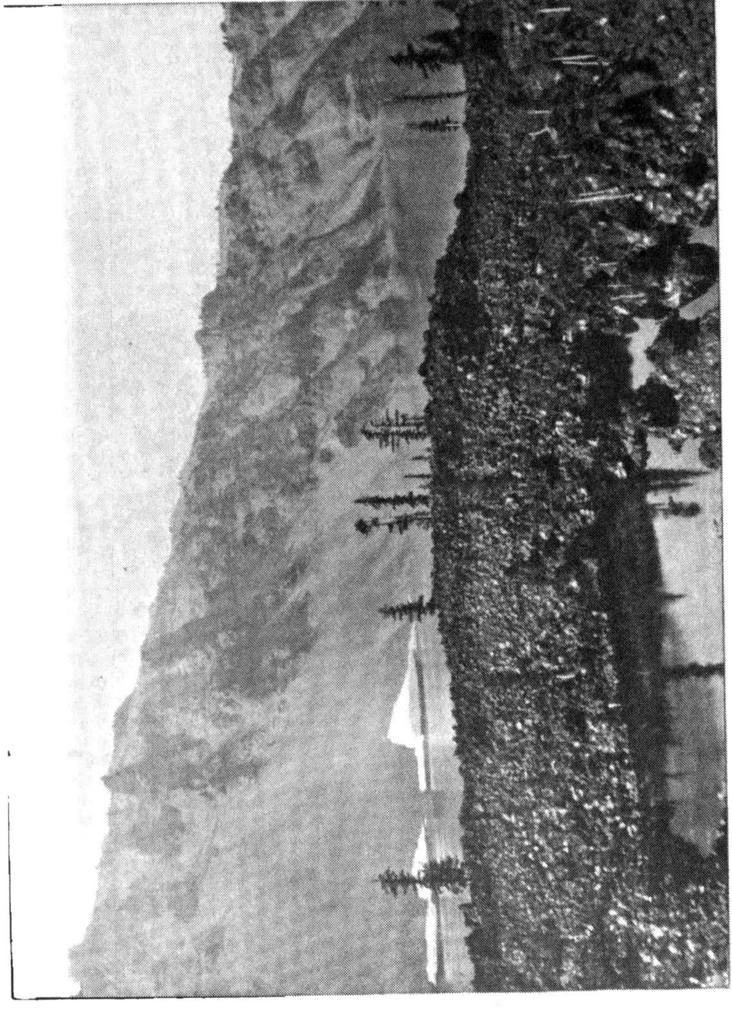

Fig. 18.—Northwestern Portion of Lava Field on Wizard Island

From a photograph by H. B. Patton.